Now You're
COOKING
HEALTHY RECIPES FROM
LATIN AMERICA

GUATEMALA

Amie Jane Leavitt

PURPLE TOAD
PUBLISHING

P.O. Box 631
Kennett Square, Pennsylvania 19348
www.purpletoadpublishing.com

Now You're COOKING
HEALTHY RECIPES FROM LATIN AMERICA

Brazil

Cuba

Guatemala

Mexico

Puerto Rico

Printing   1   2   3   4   5   6   7   8   9

Publisher's Cataloging-in-Publication Data
Leavitt, Amie Jane
  Now You're Cooking: Guatemala / Amie Jane Leavitt
    p. cm.—(Now you're cooking. Healthy recipes from Latin America)
Includes bibliographic references and index.
ISBN: 978-1-62469-038-9 (library bound)
1. Cooking, Guatemalan. 2. Cooking—Juvenile literature. 3. Recipes for health.   I. Title.
  TX716.G8 2013
  641.597281—dc23
                                    20139306073

eBook ISBN: 9781624690396

Printed by Lake Book Manufacturing, Chicago, IL

CONTENTS

Introduction

Welcome to Guatemala!

Situated in the heart of Central America, Guatemala is tucked in between the countries of Mexico, Belize, El Salvador, and Honduras. This tropical nation has coasts on both shores: the Caribbean Sea in the east and Pacific Ocean in the west. Most of Guatemala is mountainous with lush green rainforests and misty clouds that hang over them. Guatemala also has twenty-two volcanoes. Five of them are active: Pacaya erupted in 2010 and Fuego erupted in 2012. The rest of the country has beautiful white sand beaches with swaying palms and warm aqua blue water. There's also an area of the country that has a large natural lake, Lake Atitlán, that was formed when a volcano erupted and collapsed 84,000 years ago. It is over 1,000 feet deep making it the deepest lake in Central America. Small villages surround the lake, many of which are only accessible by personal boat or water taxi.

There are over fourteen million people living in Guatemala today. It is the native home of the Maya people. The ancient Mayas had a very successful civilization there from 2000 BCE until around 900 CE. There are remnants of this ancient world all over the country's highland

Tikal was the largest city of the ancient Mayan world. Six large pyramids still stand there, built somewhere between 300 BCE and 900 CE.

Guatemala

region. One of the most noteworthy Mayan ruins is called Tikal. This ancient city is located deep within the jungles of Guatemala. Tucked into dense foliage of the jungle are the remains of public squares, stone palaces, and other dwellings along with the tallest pyramid-shaped temple in all of the Americas.

The Maya people aren't the only ones who have lived in Guatemala. Spanish explorers arrived there in the early 1500s and eventually brought European settlers to the area. Today, many of the people living in Guatemala are either solely of Mayan descent or are of both Mayan and Spanish descent. Africans, Chinese, and people from other European and South American countries have settled there, too.

The food of Guatemala has been influenced by all of the people who have lived there. The Mayas ate mainly maize and black beans and the fruits and vegetables of the land. Those are still very much a part of Guatemalan cuisine. The Spanish brought with them a variety of dishes including tortillas, enchiladas, guacamole, and tamales. These dishes have taken on a uniqueness in Guatemala making them slightly different from dishes of the same name in neighboring countries. Dishes from other cultures have gained popularity there, too. In just about every town and city in Guatemala there are Chinese restaurants. A dish that has become a favorite, especially in urban areas, is the Chow Mein Tostada. This Guatemalan-Chinese dish is made by placing chow mein noodles on a crispy tostada and topping it with ketchup, soy sauce, and cheese. The Guatemalans also make their own version of pizza. Mayan pizzas are made using a special type of filled tortilla called a pupusa that is covered with cheese.

So, has all this talk of food made you hungry? If so, let's get started making some delicious Guatemalan food!

Licuados

Licuados is a fruit smoothie that can be made with many different fruits. According to native Guatemalans and people who travel to the country often, this drink defines the Guatemalan experience. It is sold just about everywhere in Guatemala: in fancy restaurants, at little comedors (inexpensive cafes), and even by street vendors.

Ingredients

1   mango, peeled, seeded, and diced
1½   cups milk
3   tablespoons honey
1   cup ice cubes

Directions

1. Place all ingredients into a blender.
2. Cover and blend until smooth.
3. Serve cold with a straw.

Serves 2

Licuados

Try making this yummy smoothie with other fruits like pineapples, bananas, papayas, strawberries, peaches, or kiwis.

Atol de Platano

Plantains, cousins of bananas, are an important part of Guatemalan cuisine. For hundreds of years, banana and coffee plantations made up the largest portion of Guatemala's economy. Bananas and plantains are also important in other countries in Central America and the Caribbean, too. Plantains are baked, fried, mashed, and mixed into dishes. For this recipe, the plantain is turned into a hot, banana-flavored drink which is perfect for a chilly winter's day in Guatemala's highland region.

Ingredients

2	ripe plantains (ripe = yellow peel with black spots)
6	cups water
1	cinnamon stick
1	allspice seed
½	cup honey

Atol de Platano

Directions

1. Peel plantains. Throw away peels.
2. Cut plantains into large chunks.
3. Place plantains, cinnamon sticks, allspice seed, and water into a medium-sized pot.
4. Bring to a boil and continue to cook for 10 minutes.
5. Remove cinnamon sticks and allspice seed from pot.
6. Scoop plantain out of water. Do not discard water.
7. Blend plantain pieces in a blender until smooth.
8. Return blended plantain to water. Cook for 10 more minutes.
9. Serve hot in mugs.

Serves 4

Atolillo

Although Guatemala is in a tropical location near the Equator, it still gets chilly in the highlands during the winter months. Because of that, beginning in November, street vendors often sell warm drinks like this one. Atolillo is a warm drink made with rice, honey, milk, and cinnamon. It is similar to eggnog. A variation can also be made with chocolate. Just like in other Latin American countries, chocolate is a popular ingredient. After all, Latin America is the home of the cacao bean that chocolate is made from.

Ingredients

½ cup brown rice
¾ cup water
1½ cups honey
6 cups milk
2 tablespoons cornstarch
1 cinnamon stick
  ground cinnamon to taste

Atolillo

Directions

1. Soak rice in water for at least 1 hour.
2. Place rice and water in blender. Blend until smooth.
3. Pour rice and water mixture and milk into a medium-sized pot.
4. Add cinnamon stick, honey, and cornstarch.
5. Cook over low heat, stirring constantly for about 30 minutes until it starts to boil and slightly thicken.
6. Taste. If it needs more cinnamon or honey, add some now.
7. Serve warm or cold in mugs.

Serves 6

You can also add cocoa powder (to taste) to the mix and you will have atol de arroz con chocolate.

Ponche de Frutas

(Fruit Punch)

It is tradition in Guatemala to make a special punch for Christmas Eve dinner and serve it with a meal of homemade tamales. Drinking ponche is believed to be a tradition that was started by the Persian people thousands of years ago. It was brought to Europe and eventually to America by the Spaniards. People in many Latin American countries drink this fruit beverage, and each country makes it slightly differently. In Guatemala, the people often include papayas and mangoes in their fruit punch.

Ingredients

1 box of raisins, soaked in water
½ cup dried apricots
½ cup dried prunes
½ cup dried apples, or one fresh apple cut into small pieces
1 pineapple
1 small papaya or dried papaya (optional)
2 sticks cinnamon
1 teaspoon allspice
1 teaspoon cloves
  Peel from one orange
  Honey, to taste
10 cups water

Directions

1. Chop dried fruit.
2. Finely chop pineapple and papaya.
3. Put all the fruit in a large cooking pot and cover with water.
4. Add spices.
5. Bring to a boil. Then, reduce heat and simmer in a covered pot for 45 minutes.

Ponche de Frutas

6. Remove from heat and add honey to taste. You will need more or less honey depending on the ripeness of the fruit. The riper the fruit, the less honey will be needed.
7. Fill cups with punch and fruit.
8. Serve with spoons.

Serves 10

Hot Christmas Punch

Christmas Punch

Ingredients

8   cups apple juice
8   cups cranberry juice
5   cinnamon sticks, broken
5   oranges, sliced ¼-inch thick

Directions

1.   Place all ingredients into large pot.
2.   Bring to a boil.
3.   Reduce heat. Let simmer for 45 minutes to one hour.
4.   Strain to remove oranges and cinnamon sticks.
5.   Serve hot in mugs.

Serves 8

Holidays in Guatemala

Holidays are important in Guatemala, especially Christmas, Easter, and the Day of the Dead.

Christmas is generally a time spent at home with family eating homemade food. Tamales are one of the most popular dishes for Christmas Eve dinner and Christmas Day breakfast. This dish is time-consuming. That's why homemade ones are often reserved for special occasions like Christmas. Tamales in Guatemala are made differently than they are in Mexico. In Mexico, this dish is made by taking a meat filling and wrapping it in corn husks. In Guatemala, a meat filling is wrapped in banana leaves. Other cuisine served at Christmastime includes chiles rellenos, hot fruit punch, hot chocolate, grapes, and apples (which are two fruits uncommon in Guatemala). Fireworks are also a big part of the celebration as is the display of the Nativity. Guatemalans put out their Nativity scenes on December 15, yet they do not place the baby Jesus in the manger until Christmas Day since that's the day they celebrate his birth.

Easter is a time of community celebration and much of the Holy Week, Semana Santa, is spent outdoors in the city. This week-long celebration is the largest of its kind anywhere in the world. The largest parades are held in the colonial city of Antigua. Beautifully decorated floats are carried down the streets by barefoot people wearing dark purple clothing and cone-shaped caps. These people are called cucuruchos. They carry the

Day of the Dead Kite Festival

floats as a way of repenting of their sins. One popular food of Easter is curtido. It's a mixture of pickled chopped vegetables. It can be served with hardboiled eggs or on top of a Guatemalan enchilada. Since so much time is spent out on the city streets, quick food from vendors is most often eaten during this special holiday. Torrejas are popular. They are similar to French toast except they're usually deep-fried. Tostadas with guacamol and cheese are also very popular.

The Day of the Dead, or El Día de los Muertos, is on November 1 every year. This holiday is extremely popular in Guatemala as it is in other Latin American countries. It is a time when extended families get together and celebrate the lives of their departed ancestors. Often times, the families will make a big picnic and go to the cemetery and eat the food by their family members' graves. The idea is that they are sharing their meal with the dead. Because of that, they want to make sure they bring food that they'll like. That is how the famous dish fiambre came to be. It is a huge salad made of almost fifty ingredients! They include cold cuts, eggs, red beets (curtido), capers, cabbage, baby corn, chorizo (sausage), heart of palm, shrimp, lettuce, cheese, and so on. It can take days to prepare, and so family members work together to get the job done. For this holiday, kids celebrate by flying colorful kites. In some towns, giant kites are flown in grand festivals.

Most of the people in Guatemala are Roman Catholic.

Breakfast

A traditional Guatemalan breakfast includes a combination of these menu items. Individual dishes are all served together in a specific way. Here's how to do it!

Ingredients

prepared black beans
baked plantains
fresh cheese
eggs, fried or scrambled
spicy red tomato sauce
spicy green tomatillo sauce
tortillas or french rolls
fresh fruit
hot chocolate or coffee

Directions

1. On a large plate, place scrambled or fried eggs.
2. Pour green sauce on one side of the eggs and red sauce on the other.
3. Scoop some prepared black beans next to eggs.
4. Place a slice of fresh cheese next to beans.
5. Scoop some baked plantains next to cheese.
6. Place tortilla or French roll on plate.
7. Add fresh fruit.
8. Serve with hot chocolate or coffee.

Breakfast is an important meal in Guatemala.

Guacamol

Avocados are an important fruit of Latin America. Because of that, each country has its own special way of using them. Nearly all of the countries make a form of guacamole, or spicy avocado dip. In Guatemala, this dip is spelled "guacamol," without the "e" on the end as the word is spelled in Mexico. It is served with tortilla chips or on top of other dishes such as tacos, enchiladas, and even in soups.

Ingredients
2   ripe avocados, peeled
1   small tomato, diced
¼   cup white onion, finely
     chopped
1   fresh green chile, chopped
⅛   cup fresh cilantro, chopped
1   lime, juiced
     salt and pepper to taste

Avocados

Directions

1. Place avocado in a small bowl. Mash with a fork.
2. Mix in other ingredients.
3. Taste. Add salt, pepper, and more lime juice if needed.
4. Serve with chips, or on entrées like tacos, enchiladas, or in soups.

Serves 2-4

If you like guacamol spicier, add more fresh green chiles.

Guacamol is a popular dish in many countries, not just in Guatemala. Its main ingredient is avocado.

Elotes Locos

These snacks are popular in Guatemala, especially at county and town fairs. Basically, they're just corn on the cob that has been topped with a variety of ingredients like grated cheese, mayonnaise, ketchup, hot sauce, hot pepper powder, and mustard. Some people push a wooden stick into one end of the corn so they don't get messy while eating it. Other people just dig in and don't care about the mess. How will you eat your elotes locos? Will you be messy or neat?

Ingredients

12 ears of corn
    mustard
    fat-free mayonnaise
    ketchup
1½ cups coarsely grated queso blanco or Parmigiano Reggiano®
    cayenne or chili pepper
    ground cumin
    fresh lime juice
    sea salt

Directions

1. Shuck corn. Throw away silk and husks.
2. Cook corn by either grilling it over a medium-heated grill or boiling it in a large pot of water. If grilling, cook until corn is tender and browned. If boiling, cook until corn is tender and bright yellow.
3. When done cooking, place corn on a large platter.
4. Sprinkle with cheese.
5. Let each person add their own toppings (mayonnaise, mustard, ketchup, cayenne pepper, lime wedges, sea salt)

Serves 12

Elotes locos are a fancy way of eating corn on the cob.

Oven-Baked Sweet Plantains

As mentioned before in the recipe for the plantain drink, plantains, as well as bananas in general, are a staple in Central America. They're served with just about every meal and are included in snacks and desserts, too. Here's how to eat them in a super sweet way as a side dish to one of your favorite Guatemalan dishes (like tacos, enchiladas, or pepián).

Ingredients

4   very ripe plantains (peel should be yellow with black spots)

Directions

1. Preheat oven to 450°F.
2. Spray a cooking sheet with cooking spray.
3. Peel plantains and cut ends off.
4. Cut each plantain into ½-inch diagonal slices.
5. Place plantain slices on sheet in a single layer.
6. Spray with a little more cooking spray.
7. As plantains bake, turn them occasionally.
8. Bake for 10–15 minutes until plantains are tender and golden brown.

Serves 4-6

Baked plantains

These are served as a side dish at any meal.

Picado de Rábano
(Radish Salad)

Fresh produce is essential to the Guatemalan diet. Some of the most popular vegetables are yucca, carrots, celery, cucumbers, and radishes. All of these help make the Guatemalan diet generally healthy. This particular recipe for radish salad is a popular side dish. It tastes extra fresh with a light dressing of orange and lemon juice.

Ingredients

½   pound radishes (about 20)
12 fresh mint leaves, finely chopped
⅓   cup orange juice
¼   cup lemon juice
    salt, to taste

Directions

1. Trim ends off radishes.
2. Slice radishes into thin slices.
3. Combine sliced radishes with mint leaves, salt, and citrus juices.
4. Serve in small bowls.

Serves 2-4

Radishes can be chopped.

Plants and Animals of Guatemala

Most of Guatemala is tropical rainforest. That means plant and animal life are abundant there.

Some plants that are native to Guatemala are:

- cacao (chocolate)
- coconut
- avocado
- papaya
- dragon fruit
- sugar apple
- breadfruit
- zapote
- guava
- Indian fig
- monkey apple
- pineapple
- mango
- starfruit

Some animals that are native to Guatemala are:

- macaws (parrots)
- toucans
- hummingbirds
- trogons
- quetzals (Guatemala's national bird that is endangered)
- jaguars
- howler monkeys
- tapirs
- kinkajous
- manatees
- crocodiles
- turtles
- red-eyed tree frogs

Jaguars are native to Guatemala. These powerful predators once roamed most of South America and part of North America. Today, they are only found in a few select locations.

Pepián

Many people consider pepián to be the national dish of Guatemala. It is served in just about every region of the country. This dish is a blend of the Mayan and European cultures. Pepián is usually made with chicken, and Guatemalans serve it over rice and have a basket of warm tortillas on the side. You can use the tortillas like bread to soak up any of the remaining sauce in your bowl.

Ingredients

3	cups tomatoes, chopped
2	red bell peppers, chopped
1	cup green beans
1	chayote, chopped
1	poblano pepper, chopped
1	jalapeno pepper, chopped
1	onion, diced
1	clove garlic, minced
4	ounces squash seeds
4	ounces sesame seeds
4	cups chicken, cubed
2	cups potatoes, cubed
2	carrots, diced
2	cups brown rice, cooked
1	bunch cilantro
	salt
	pepper
4	tortillas

Directions

1. In a medium pot, cook chicken, onion, and garlic in a small amount of olive oil. Cook until meat is cooked all the way through.

Stews are served with warm tortillas in Guatemala instead of bread.

2. Add carrots, potatoes, and green beans. Simmer until all vegetables are tender.
3. On a baking sheet, roast tomatoes, peppers, squash seeds, and sesame seeds in a 400°F oven. Let cool. Then, blend these ingredients in a blender until smooth.
4. Add blended ingredients to meat mixture.
5. Season to taste with salt and pepper.
6. Serve over brown rice with tortillas on the side.

Serves 4-6

Guatemalan
Enchiladas

In Guatemala, enchiladas are different from those in Mexico. Guatemalan enchiladas are more like Mexican tostadas, with a twist. They are topped with many interesting ingredients including a mixture of pickled beets and cabbage (curtido). These are popular any time of year, but especially during Easter. Here is how to make curtido-topped enchiladas

Ingredients for curtido
2 cups cabbage, shredded
½ cup carrot, shredded
1 large beet, peeled and shredded
1 red bell pepper, sliced finely
2 onions, sliced
3 cloves garlic, chopped
2 bay leaves
1 cup vinegar
1 cup olive oil
thyme, optional
mustard powder, optional

Ingredients for enchilada
6 corn shells, sprayed lightly with cooking spray and baked in
    an oven until crispy
lettuce, chopped
curtido (see recipe below)
1 cup cooked chicken, shredded
3 eggs, hardboiled and sliced
parsley, chopped
hard cheese, like Parmesan
salsa

**A slide of hard bolied egg
makes for an attractive garnish.**

Directions to make curtido
1. Cook onions and garlic until clear and soft.
2. Cook cabbage and carrot in a little water until soft.
3. Cook beet and red bell pepper together until soft.
4. Drain all vegetables and toss together with bay leaves, vinegar, and olive oil.
5. You may add a dash of mustard powder or thyme, as well.
6. Let mixture sit overnight in refrigerator.

Directions to make enchilada
1. Sprinkle lettuce on crunchy corn shells (tostadas).
2. Scoop on some curtido, then chicken, and then salsa, egg, parsley, and cheese. Serve warm.

Serves 6

Coconut Rice and Beans

Just as in many Latin American countries, rice and beans accompany just about every meal in Guatemala. In fact, for some people, this dish may be the entire meal. Rice and beans are very nutritious and a good source of protein. This recipe adds an ingredient which is plentiful in Guatemala: coconut milk.

Ingredients

2   cups black beans, dry
2   cloves garlic
1   teaspoon salt
1   cup coconut milk
½   teaspoon black pepper
½   teaspoon thyme
2   cups brown rice, dry
1   medium onion, diced
16 cups water

Directions

1. Wash beans thoroughly.
2. Place beans in a large bowl and soak for at least four hours in at least 8 cups water.
3. After soaking beans, strain off water.
4. Place them in a medium-sized cooking pot with 8 more cups water. Add onions and garlic. Boil the beans until they are tender.
5. Once tender, season beans with black pepper, thyme, and salt.
6. Add coconut milk. Stir and return to a boil.
7. Add dry rice. Stir, then cover. Cook on low heat until all the water is absorbed and rice is tender. If necessary, add more water gradually.

Serves 4-6

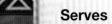

Rice and beans
are a staple
food source for
many people in
Central and
South America.

Chiles Rellenos

Chiles rellenos are made throughout Latin America. This dish is particularly popular in Guatemala at Christmastime. Chiles rellenos are usually fried; however, baking them is a healthier option.

Ingredients

6 canned whole green chiles
6 slices Monterey Jack cheese
6 slices cheddar cheese
flour
8 eggs, separated
¼ cup olive oil
picante sauce

Directions

1. Drain water from chiles.
2. Place them on a large cutting board.
3. Cut a slit in one side of each chile.
4. Insert one strip of Jack cheese and one strip of cheddar cheese inside each chile.
5. Dust chiles with flour.
6. Beat egg whites until stiff.
7. Beat egg yolks and fold into egg whites.
8. Add oil to egg mixture. You have just made an egg batter.
9. Spray an 8 x 8 baking dish with cooking spray.
10. Pour a thick coating of batter on bottom of dish.
11. Place chiles on top of batter.
12. Spoon remaining batter over chiles.
13. Bake at 375°F for 15 minutes.
14. Top with picante sauce and serve.

Serves 6

Chiles rellenos is a delightful dish that's both slightly salty and spicy.

Arroz Guatemalteco

Rice is served as both a side dish and main dish in Guatemala. This dish is a favorite in Guatemala because it includes a unique flavoring of chicken broth and a mixture of finely chopped vegetables.

Ingredients
2   cups brown rice
2   tablespoons oil
1   cup mixed vegetables (carrots, celery, sweet red peppers, green peas), finely chopped
    Salt and pepper, to taste
4   cups chicken stock

Directions
1. Heat oil in a medium pot.
2. Add rice.
3. Sauté lightly until rice absorbs oil. Stir constantly so it doesn't burn.
4. Add mixed vegetables, salt, pepper, and chicken stock.
5. Bring to a boil. Cover with a lid and reduce heat to low.
6. Cool for about 20 minutes or until liquid has absorbed and rice is tender.

Serves 6

Arroz
Guatemalteco

Guatemalan Tacos

Just as Guatemalan enchiladas differ from those of Mexico, so do Guatemalan tacos. They look more like Mexican taquitos than tacos. Their filling is uniquely Guatemalan, too. It includes potatoes along with meat to make for a heartier meal. There's also a tasty avocado and jalapeño sauce that is poured on top.

Ingredients

5   large potatoes, cubed and cooked
1   pound ground turkey
½   onion, chopped
    salt and pepper, to taste
4   tomatillos, husked and quartered
1   garlic clove, peeled
1   jalapeño pepper, diced
½   cup fresh cilantro, chopped
3   avocados, peeled with pits removed
20 (6-inch) corn tortillas

Directions

1. Crumble ground turkey into a skillet. Add onion.
2. Cook over medium-high heat until meat is no longer pink and onion is tender.
3. Gently stir in cooked potatoes.
4. Season with salt and pepper to taste.
5. Place avocados, tomatillos, garlic, jalapeño, and cilantro into a blender.
6. Blend until smooth.

7. Heat tortillas in microwave or in a warm skillet until warm and flexible.
8. Spoon about two teaspoons of meat mixture on one end of each tortilla.
9. Roll tightly into tubes.
10. Place them on a baking sheet. Bake for 10 minutes in a 400°F oven or until crispy.
11. Place several on a plate, top with sauce, and serve.

Serves 5-8

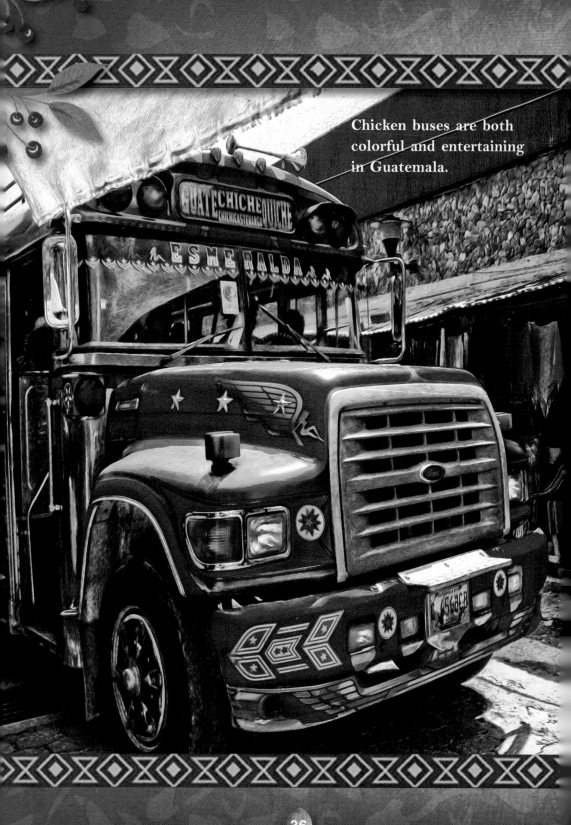

Chicken buses are both colorful and entertaining in Guatemala.

Transportation in Guatemala

Only a third of the people in Guatemala own their own cars. Most just walk from place to place, even in rural areas. Some people ride bikes. Others ride public buses called camionetas, or "chicken buses."

Where do these buses come from?

When school buses in the United States are a certain age or have been driven for so many miles, they are retired. These retired buses are often bought by other countries to use for public transportation. That's where many of the "chicken buses" in Guatemala come from. The old yellow paint is covered up with bright red, green, blue, and aqua paint. Some even have colorful murals depicting religious images. Racks are placed on top of the buses to hold luggage. The reason they are called "chicken buses" is because in rural areas, people often bring their livestock aboard. After all, if you need to get your animals from one place to another and you don't have a vehicle of your own, a public bus is a good way to do it!

Guatemalan Pan de Banana
(Banana Bread)

Rich desserts aren't common in Guatemala. That's probably because of the fresh fruit available all year long that can satisfy a person's sweet tooth. Breads are popular though, especially pan de banana or banana bread. This bread can be eaten plain, or it can be served with honey drizzled on top. This particular recipe is a healthier alternative to traditional banana bread. The butter and sugar have been replaced with applesauce and honey.

Ingredients

3 ripe bananas (peels should be black)
1 cup honey
½ cup applesauce
2 eggs
1 teaspoon baking soda
1 teaspoon baking powder
1 teaspoon salt
1 teaspoon vanilla extract
2 cups flour (can be whole grain)

Directions

1. On a plate, smash bananas with a fork.
2. Stir in honey and let stand for 15 minutes.
3. Add applesauce and eggs. Beat well with an electric hand mixer.
4. Add baking soda, baking powder, salt, and vanilla. Mix well.
5. Slowly add in flour. Mix well.
6. Pour into a 9 x 5-inch loaf pan that has been coated with nonstick spray.

Banana bread is a favorite
in many cultures.

7. Bake at 350°F for 45 minutes or until a toothpick inserted in the center of the loaf comes out clean.
8. Remove from oven.
9. Let stand for 10 minutes before removing from pan.
10. Serve slices either plain or with honey drizzled on top.

Makes 1 loaf

Lemon, Banana, and Mango Cupsicle

You have probably heard of popsicles, right? Well, this recipe shows you how to make something similar—a frozen treat called a "cupsicle" that is popular in Guatemala. These concoctions got their name from the small paper cups Guatemalans use to make them. The fruit used in this recipe are typical of Guatemala. If you prefer, though, you can exchange them for other fruits that might be more available in your area like peaches, strawberries, passion fruit, watermelon, or pineapple.

Ingredients

2   ripe mangoes, peeled, seeded, and mashed
1   ripe banana, peeled and mashed
1   cup thick Greek yogurt
1   tablespoon lemon juice
6   small paper Dixie® cups
    wooden popsicle sticks (unused)

cupsicles

Directions

1. In a small bowl, mix all ingredients together.
2. Scoop mixture ¾ up into paper cups.
3. Add popsicle stick to the center of each cup.
4. Freeze for at least 3 hours.
5. To eat, peel away paper and enjoy!

Makes 6

Canillitas
de Leches
(Milk Candies)

Kids living in Guatemala definitely know what canillitas de leches are. They're often sold in small bags in marketplaces. These milk candies are a traditional Guatemalan sweet treat.

Ingredients
½ cup honey
4 cups powdered milk
1½ cans (14-ounce) fat-free, sweetened condensed milk
1 teaspoon vanilla extract
½ cup powdered sugar
   cornstarch (for kneading)

Directions

Milk candy

1. Place all ingredients except cornstarch in a bowl.
2. Use an electric hand mixer to mix on low for 30 seconds.
3. Then, mix on medium for 1 minute or until mix is a stiff consistency.
4. Dust a clean cutting board with a little cornstarch.
5. Place dough on cutting board.
6. Knead dough for a minute with hands. Use more cornstarch on hands if dough starts to stick.
7. Use a rolling pin and roll mixture out onto board. Then, cut into different shapes using cookie cutters. Dust with cornstarch as you go if it gets sticky.
8. Wrap shapes in cellophane to store.

Makes 24 pieces

Bocado de Reina Cake

This cake is made using leftover bread. It's name means "bite of a queen." This means the cake is supposed to be so delicious that it's fit for a queen. People in Guatemala try not to throw out anything. This cake is how they make sure that even older bread is used.

Ingredients

2 cups of crumbled bread (any kind you have)
1 can fat-free, sweetened condensed milk
2 eggs
1 tablespoon cinnamon
2 bananas
  raisins (optional)

Directions

1. Mix all ingredients together in a large bowl.
2. Spray an 8-inch round or square cake pan with cooking spray.
3. Place bread mixture in pan.
4. Bake at 350°F for 45 minutes.

Serves 4-6

Bocada de Reina Cake can
be served with ice cream or
frozen yogurt.

Books

Aboff, Marcie. *Guatemala ABCs: A Book About the People and Places of Guatemala.* Mankato, MN: Picture Window Books, 2003.

Englar, Mary. *Guatemala: A Question and Answer Book.* Mankato, MN: Capstone, 2005.

Knudsen, Shannon. *Guatemala: Country Explorers.* Minneapolis, MN: Lerner Classroom, 2011.

Stalcup, Ann. *Mayan Weaving: A Living Tradition (Crafts of the World).* New York: PowerKids Press, 2003.

Villatoro, Marina K. *Guatemala, A Family Travel Guide.* (Kindle Edition). Amazon Digital Services, 2012.

Works Consulted

Antigua Daily Photo, http://antiguadailyphoto.com/

Fodor's Guatemala Travel Guide, http://www.fodors.com/world/mexico-and-central-america/guatemala/

Frommer's Guatemala, http://www.frommers.com/destinations/guatemala/

Growing Up Bilingual, http://growingupbilingual.com

Guatemalan Fiambre, http://www.saveur.com/article/Travels/Guatemalan-Fiambre

Lonely Planet's Guatemala, http://www.lonelyplanet.com/guatemala

You Only Live Once (blog), http://cadaut.blogspot.com/p/year-in-guatemala.html

On the Internet

Kids Discover Magazine, The Maya

www.kidsdiscover.com/maya-for-kids

Kids National Geographic, Guatemala

www.kids.nationalgeographic.com/kids/places/find/guatemala/

National Geographic, Guatemala

http://travel.nationalgeographic.com/travel/countries/guatemala-guide/

World Factbook (CIA), Guatemala

https://www.cia.gov/library/publications/the-world-factbook/geos/gt.html

camionetas (kam-ee-oh-NEH-tuhs)—Old school buses purchased from the United States that are used for public transportation. Also known as "chicken buses."

cellophane (SEH-luh-fayn)—Thin, clear material used to cover food to keep it fresh.

chiles rellenos (CHEE-lays ree-YAY-nohs)—Stuffed chile peppers that are usually fried.

curtido (ker-TEE-doh)—Pickled beet and cabbage salad commonly eaten at Easter and on Guatemalan enchiladas.

knead (NEED)—To work dough with your hands by folding, pressing, and stretching it.

pupusa (pooh-POOH-suh)—A tortilla-like dish made using maize and filled with meats or cheeses, then grilled or fried.

tostada (tohs-TAH-duh)—Fried tortilla. It can also be baked. It is usually served as a base with other ingredients on top like guacamol, meat, cheese, and the like.

tortilla (tor-TEE-uh)—A thin, corn pancake.

About the AUTHOR

Amie Jane Leavitt is an accomplished author, researcher, and photographer. She graduated from Brigham Young University as an education major and has since taught all subjects and grade levels in both private and public schools. Leavitt is an adventurer who loves to travel the globe in search of interesting story ideas and beautiful places to capture in photos. She has written over fifty books for kids, has contributed to online and print media, and has worked as a consultant, writer, and editor for numerous educational publishing and assessment companies. In addition to this cookbook, Leavitt has also written *Now You're Cooking: Healthy Recipes from Latin America (Puerto Rico)* for Purple Toad Publishing. For a list of her current projects and published works, check out Leavitt's web site at www.amiejaneleavitt.com.